THE ART OF WOOD CARVING

Unlocking The Secrets Of Wood Sculpture

Jeremy Henderson
copyright@2024

Table of Content

CHAPTER 1
- Introduction To Wood Carving
- Wood Carving
- Types of Carving

CHAPTER 2
- Essential Tools And Materials
- How To Choose The Right Wood

CHAPTER 3
- Safety Guidelines And Practices

CHAPTER 4
- Basic Wood Carving Techniques
- Whittling Technique
- Relief Carving
- Chip Carving
- Adding Finishing Touches

CHAPTER 5
- Wood Carving Projects
- Basic Whittled Spoon
- Whittled Keychain
- Whittled Bird
- Whittled Letter Opener
- Relief Carved Flower
- Relief Carved Celtic Knot
- Relief Carved Animal Silhouette

- Relief Carved Sunburst Design
- Chip Carved Coaster
- Chip Carved Wooden Box Lid
- Chip Carved Wooden Spoon Handle
- Chip Carved Decorative Plate

CHAPTER 6
- Troubleshooting
- General Tips

CONCLUSION

CHAPTER 1
Introduction To Wood Carving

Welcome to the enchanting world of wood carving, where the marriage of skill and creativity transforms a humble piece of timber into a work of art. In this guide we embark on a journey to demystify the craft, making it accessible and enjoyable for all.

Wood carving is a timeless practice that spans cultures and generations. It goes beyond a mere craft; it's an expression of artistry, patience, and a deep connection with the natural material. In this introductory chapter, we'll explore the essence of wood carving, its rich history, and the joy that comes with bringing life to wood through your hands.

Throughout this guide, we'll delve into the different realms of wood carving, from the simplicity of whittling to the intricacies of relief carving and chip carving. Whether you're a complete novice or someone looking to refine their skills, this book is designed to be your trusted companion on this creative journey.

So, grab your carving tools, find a comfortable workspace, and let the journey into the heart of wood carving begin. Discover the satisfaction of creating your own masterpieces and unlocking the artistic potential that lies within the grain of each piece of wood.

Wood Carving

Wood carving is a traditional craft and art form that involves shaping and sculpting wood using various cutting tools. Carvers use knives, chisels, gouges, and other specialized tools to remove wood material and create intricate designs, patterns, or three-dimensional sculptures. Wood carving can range from simple, utilitarian objects to highly detailed and artistic pieces.

Types of Carving

Wood carving encompasses various techniques and styles, each with its unique characteristics and applications. Here are some of the main types of carving:

1. Whittling:

Description: Whittling involves carving wood using a small, sharp knife to remove small chips or shavings. It's often associated with creating simple, hand-held items like figurines, spoons, or walking sticks.

Applications: Whittling is suitable for beginners and those who enjoy the simplicity of carving with minimal tools.

2. Relief Carving:

Description: In relief carving, a design is carved into a flat surface, creating a raised, three-dimensional image. The background is then lowered to emphasize the carved design.

Applications: Commonly used for decorative panels, furniture embellishments, and architectural details.

3. Chip Carving:

Description: Chip carving involves removing small chips of wood to create intricate geometric or stylized patterns. This technique relies on precise knife work and is often used for decorative purposes.

Applications: Commonly used for decorating wooden objects like plates, boxes, and furniture.

4. Green Wood Carving:

Description: Green wood carving involves working with fresh, unseasoned wood. The wood is easier to carve when green, and it allows for more significant shaping and sculpting.

Applications: Often used for carving large sculptures, bowls, or functional items from freshly cut wood.

5. Cane Carving:

Description: Cane carving focuses on creating intricate designs on the shaft of walking sticks or canes. The carver may incorporate relief carving, chip carving, or other techniques.

Applications: Often used for decorative walking sticks or canes, showcasing the carver's skills and creativity.

6. Sculptural Carving:

Description: Sculptural carving involves creating three-dimensional forms and figures from wood. This can range from small figurines to life-sized sculptures.

Applications: Used for creating art pieces, statues, and intricate sculptures, allowing the carver to express creativity and artistic vision.

7. Power Carving:

Description: Power carving involves using power tools like rotary tools or electric chainsaws to remove wood quickly. It's often employed for larger projects or when efficiency is crucial.

Applications: Used for carving larger sculptures, furniture components, or when speed and precision are essential.

8. Intaglio Carving:

Description: Intaglio carving involves carving into the surface of wood, creating depressions or recessed areas. This technique is often associated with printmaking, where the carved surface is used for printing.

Applications: Commonly used for creating woodblocks for printmaking, decorative panels, or intricate designs.

9. Letter Carving:

Description: Letter carving focuses on carving letters and words into wood. This can range from simple inscriptions to elaborate typography.

Applications: Used for creating signs, inscriptions, and decorative lettering on wooden surfaces.

10. Decorative Carving:

Description: Decorative carving encompasses various styles and techniques used to add embellishments, patterns, or designs to wooden surfaces. It often combines relief carving, chip carving, and other decorative elements.

Applications: Widely used for adding ornamental details to furniture, architectural elements, and crafts.

These carving techniques offer a broad range of possibilities, allowing artisans to express their creativity and skills in diverse ways. The choice of carving style often depends on the desired outcome, the carver's preferences, and the intended application of the finished piece.

CHAPTER 2
Essential Tools And Materials

The materials you need for wood carving depend on the specific carving technique and the complexity of your projects. Here's a general list of materials to get you started:

1. Wood: Choose a suitable wood based on your project and skill level. Softwoods like pine or basswood are great for beginners, while hardwoods like oak or walnut are better for more advanced carvers.

2. Carving Tools: Invest in a set of quality carving tools. A basic set may include:

- Carving knives: for whittling and fine details.
- Gouges: for scooping out wood and creating curves.
- Chisels: for straight cuts and shaping.
- V-tools: for carving V-shaped grooves.

3. Safety Gear: Ensure your safety with the following protective gear:

- Safety glasses: Wear safety glasses to shield your eyes from flying wood chips.
- Carving gloves: to protect your hands from cuts and splinters.

4. Sharpening Tools: Keep your carving tools sharp with:

- Sharpening stones or strops: for maintaining tool edges.

5. Wood Finishes: Enhance the appearance and protect your carvings with:

- Clear wood finishes: like varnish, shellac, or oil.

6. Sandpaper: Smooth the surface of your carvings with various grits of sandpaper.

7. Wood Glue: Use wood glue for assembling carved pieces or fixing mistakes.

8. Pencil and Eraser: Sketch your designs onto the wood before carving.

9. Clamps: Secure your wood to a stable surface to prevent movement while carving.

10. Wood Carving Mallet: If you're using gouges and chisels, a wooden mallet is essential for controlled strikes.

11. Carving Bench or Worktable: Have a dedicated space to work on your projects, preferably at a comfortable height.

12. Dust Mask: Protect yourself from wood dust by wearing a dust mask, especially when sanding.

13. Wood Carving Apron: Keep your clothes clean and protect yourself from wood chips with a carving apron.

14. Wood Rasp and Files: These tools are useful for refining shapes and smoothing rough areas.

15. Carving Stencils or Patterns: If you're new to carving, having pre-made patterns or stencils can guide your designs.

16. Wood Carving Book or Guide: Invest in a good wood carving book or guide to learn techniques, tips, and project ideas.

17. Palette or Mixing Tray (for finishes): If you're using finishes, have a palette or mixing tray for application.

Remember that the specific materials you need can vary based on the type of carving you're doing. As you gain more experience, you may find that you prefer certain tools or finishes over others. It's also a good idea to build your collection gradually as you take on more complex projects.

How To Choose The Right Wood

Choosing the right wood for your carving projects is a crucial step in ensuring a successful and enjoyable wood carving experience. Here are some considerations to help you select the appropriate wood:

Wood Hardness: Consider the hardness of the wood species. Softer woods, such as pine, cedar, or basswood, are ideal for beginners as they are easier to carve. As you gain experience, you can explore harder woods like oak or walnut for more intricate carvings.

Grain Pattern: Examine the grain pattern of the wood. Straight, consistent grains are often easier to carve, while irregular grains may pose challenges. The grain direction affects how the wood will respond to carving tools, so understanding it is crucial for achieving desired results.

Workability: Evaluate the overall workability of the wood. Some woods are more forgiving and easier to carve than others. Consider the ease with which the wood can be shaped and detailed, especially if you are a beginner looking for a forgiving material.

Availability: Choose wood that is readily available in your region or through local suppliers. This ensures easy access to materials for your projects and helps you become familiar with the characteristics of the wood available in your area.

Cost: Be mindful of your budget. Different wood species come at varying costs, and some rare or exotic woods can be expensive. Start with more affordable options and gradually explore different woods as you progress in your carving journey.

Intended Use: Consider the intended use of the carved piece. If you're creating functional items like utensils or bowls, choose a wood that is food-safe and durable. For decorative items, prioritize aesthetics and choose a wood that complements your design.

Wood Stability: Check the stability of the wood. Some woods are prone to splitting or warping, especially if they haven't been properly seasoned. Opt for well-dried and seasoned wood to minimize potential issues during and after carving.

Experimentation: Don't be afraid to experiment with different wood types. Each wood has its unique characteristics, and exploring a variety of woods will enhance your understanding of how different species respond to carving tools.

By considering these factors, you can make informed decisions when choosing wood for your carving projects. As you gain experience, you'll develop a personal preference for certain woods based on your carving style and the specific qualities you value in the material.

CHAPTER 3
Safety Guidelines And Practices

Ensuring safety is paramount in wood carving. Follow these guidelines and practices to create a secure carving environment:

Wear Protective Gear: Always wear safety gloves to protect your hands from accidental slips or cuts.

Use eye protection, such as safety glasses or goggles, to shield your eyes from wood chips and debris generated during carving.

Consider wearing a dust mask if working with fine wood dust or for extended periods to minimize respiratory exposure.

Maintain Sharp Tools: Keep your carving tools sharp. Dull tools can lead to accidents as they may require more force to use.

Regularly sharpen tools using a sharpening stone or honing kit to ensure precise and controlled carving.

Secure Workpiece Properly: Secure your wood securely in a stable workbench or clamp it down. This prevents the wood from slipping during carving, reducing the risk of accidents.

Carve Away from Your Body: Always carve away from your body, keeping your hands and body out of the path of the carving tool. This minimizes the risk of self-injury.

Mind Your Surroundings: Carve in a well-lit and well-ventilated space.

Remove clutter from your workspace to prevent tripping hazards.

Learn Proper Tool Handling: Familiarize yourself with proper tool handling techniques. Understand the correct way to hold and control your carving knife, chisels, and gouges.

Start with Simple Projects: Begin with simple and manageable projects, especially if you are a beginner. This helps you develop basic carving skills before tackling more complex designs.

Take Breaks: Carving can be physically demanding. Take regular breaks to prevent fatigue, which can compromise your focus and coordination.

Educate Yourself: Educate yourself on the characteristics of the wood you're carving.

Different woods have unique properties that can affect carving techniques and safety.

Dispose of Waste Safely: Dispose of wood scraps and waste in a safe manner. Maintain an organized workspace to minimize the likelihood of accidents.

Have a First Aid Kit: Keep a well-equipped first aid kit nearby in case of minor injuries. Be prepared to address cuts, abrasions, or other small wounds promptly.

By adhering to these safety guidelines and practices, you create a safer environment for your wood carving pursuits, allowing you to enjoy the craft with confidence and peace of mind.

CHAPTER 4
Basic Wood Carving Techniques

Whittling Technique

Step 1: Gather Your Materials

Collect your whittling materials, including a softwood block (such as pine or cedar) and a sharp carving knife.

Step 2: Select a Comfortable Workspace

Choose a well-lit and well-ventilated workspace with a stable surface. Make sure there is ample space for unrestricted arm movement.

Step 3: Choose the Right Knife Grip

Hold the carving knife in a comfortable grip. The most common grip is a handshake grip, where the knife handle rests in the palm of your hand, and your thumb rests on the back of the blade.

Step 4: Practice Safe Techniques

Begin with safety in mind. Perform carving motions away from your body to prevent inadvertent injuries. Keep your fingers away from the path of the blade.

Step 5: Make a Simple Cut

Start with a simple push cut. Position the knife perpendicular to the wood and push it away from you. Control the depth of the cut with the pressure applied.

Step 6: Master the Pull Cut

Practice the pull cut by pulling the knife toward you while keeping the blade in contact with the wood. This technique is essential for shaping and refining your carving.

Step 7: Create Basic Shapes

Carve away small, controlled pieces of wood to create basic shapes. Begin with simple geometric forms to get a feel for the knife's movement and control.

Step 8: Explore Whittling Techniques

Experiment with different whittling techniques, such as notching, rounding, and chamfering. Each technique serves a purpose in creating various textures and details in your carving.

Step 9: Refine and Smooth

Refine your carving by removing any rough edges or uneven surfaces. Use your carving knife or sandpaper to smooth the wood and achieve the desired finish.

Step 10: Embrace Creativity

Let your creativity flow. As you become more comfortable with the basic whittling techniques, start incorporating curves, angles, and patterns into your carvings.

Step 11: Take Breaks and Reflect

Wood carving requires focus and patience. Take breaks when needed, step back, and reflect on your progress. This helps maintain precision and prevents fatigue.

Step 12: Finish and Protect

Once satisfied with your carving, consider applying a wood finish or sealant to enhance the wood's appearance and protect your creation.

Remember, practice is key to mastering whittling techniques. Start with simple projects, and gradually challenge yourself with more complex designs as you gain confidence and skill. Happy whittling!

Relief Carving

Step 1: Gather Your Materials

Collect your relief carving materials, including a hardwood block, carving gouges and chisels, a mallet, and sandpaper.

Step 2: Choose a Design and Transfer It

Select a design for your relief carving. Transfer the design onto the wood using tracing paper or by drawing it directly onto the surface.

Step 3: Secure the Wood

Secure the wood block firmly on a stable work surface using clamps or a vise. This ensures stability and safety during the carving process.

Step 4: Outline the Design

Use a fine carving tool to outline the main elements of your design. This creates a guide for the deeper carving that will follow.

Step 5: Establish Levels

Identify different levels within your design. Begin carving away the background areas first, establishing the base level for your relief.

Step 6: Use Gouges for Depth

Select appropriate gouges to create depth and detail in your relief. Larger gouges remove more material, while smaller ones are ideal for intricate details.

Step 7: Work from Background to Foreground

Carve from the background toward the foreground, gradually bringing elements of your design forward. This layering creates a three-dimensional effect.

Step 8: Be Mindful of Grain Direction

Take note of the wood's grain direction. Carve in the same direction as the grain to prevent splintering and achieve smoother results.

Step 9: Refine and Detail

Refine your relief carving by adding finer details and smoothing surfaces. Use smaller chisels and carving tools to capture intricate elements.

Step 10: Sand the Surface

Sand the carved surface using progressively finer grits of sandpaper. This step helps achieve a polished and smooth finish, enhancing the visual appeal of your relief carving.

Step 11: Finish and Protect

Consider applying a wood finish or sealant to enhance the wood's appearance and protect your relief carving. Choose a finish that complements the type of wood you've used.

Step 12: Reflect and Enjoy

Step back and admire your relief carving. Take a moment to reflect on the details and the overall design. Celebrate your accomplishment!

Relief carving requires patience and precision, so take your time and enjoy the creative process. As you become more proficient, you can explore more intricate designs and refine your skills in capturing depth and dimension within the wood. Happy carving!

Chip Carving
Step 1: Gather Your Materials

Collect your chip carving materials, including a softwood block (such as basswood or butternut), chip carving knives, a pencil, ruler, and possibly a stencil or pattern.

Step 2: Choose a Design

Select a simple geometric design or pattern for your chip carving. This can be a traditional motif or your own creation. Sketch the design on paper if needed.

Step 3: Transfer the Design

Transfer your chosen design onto the wood using a pencil. You can use a stencil or draw the design freehand. Ensure the lines are clear and well-defined.

Step 4: Mark the Positive and Negative Spaces

Identify the positive spaces (areas to be carved) and negative spaces (areas to be retained) in your design. Mark these areas on the wood with a pencil to guide your carving.

Step 5: Secure the Wood

Secure the wood block on a stable work surface using clamps or a vise. This ensures stability and safety during the carving process.

Step 6: Begin with Straight Cuts

Use the chip carving knife to make straight cuts along the design lines. Start with shallow cuts, gradually increasing the depth as needed. Focus on creating clean, straight lines.

Step 7: Execute Angled Cuts

Introduce angled cuts to create triangular chips. These cuts should meet at the design lines, forming V-shaped notches. Maintain consistency in the angle and depth of your cuts.

Step 8: Work from the Center Outward

Start carving from the center of your design and work outward. This helps maintain symmetry and balance in your chip carving.

Step 9: Manage Grain Direction

Take note of the wood's grain direction. Adjust the angle of your cuts to accommodate the grain, preventing splintering and achieving cleaner results.

Step 10: Detail and Refine

Add finer details and refine your chip carving by adjusting the depth of individual chips. This step allows you to create depth and texture within the design.

Step 11: Clean Up Edges

Use the chip carving knife to clean up any rough edges and ensure the design lines are crisp. This step contributes to the overall polished appearance of your chip carving.

Step 12: Sand and Finish

Sand the carved surface using fine-grit sandpaper to smooth any remaining roughness. Consider applying a wood finish or sealant to protect your chip carving and enhance its visual appeal.

Step 13: Reflect and Appreciate

Step back, reflect on your chip carving, and appreciate the intricacies of the design. Celebrate your accomplishment and the artistry created through the interplay of positive and negative spaces.

Chip carving requires practice and precision, so take your time to develop your skills. As you become more comfortable with the technique, you can experiment with more complex patterns and designs. Enjoy the creative process!

Adding Finishing Touches

Adding finishing touches to your wood carving enhances its overall appearance and ensures a polished, professional result. Here's a step-by-step guide on how to add those final details:

Step 1: Evaluate Your Carving

Step back and carefully examine your carving. Identify any rough spots, uneven surfaces, or areas that need refinement.

Step 2: Sanding

Use fine-grit sandpaper to smooth the entire surface of your carving. Sand in the direction of the wood grain to avoid creating scratches. Focus on areas where you've made cuts or removed material to achieve a consistent, polished finish.

Step 3: Round Over Edges

Consider rounding over sharp edges to create a softer and more pleasing appearance. This can be done with a small-radius gouge, sandpaper, or even a fine file.

Step 4: Remove Dust

Wipe away any sawdust or debris from the carving using a soft, clean cloth or a brush. This step ensures that your finish adheres smoothly to the wood.

Step 5: Choose a Finish

Select an appropriate wood finish or sealant based on the type of wood you've used and your desired look. Common finishes include clear varnish, oil-based finishes, or wax. Test a small, inconspicuous area first to ensure the finish achieves the desired effect.

Step 6: Apply the Finish

Apply the chosen finish according to the manufacturer's instructions. Use a brush, cloth, or foam applicator, ensuring even coverage. Allow the finish to penetrate the wood and dry completely between coats.

Step 7: Multiple Coats (Optional)

If desired, apply multiple coats of finish to deepen the color and enhance the protective layer. Sand lightly between coats with fine-grit sandpaper for a smooth and even finish.

Step 8: Detailing (Optional)

If your carving includes intricate details, consider using a small brush to add highlights or accents with paint or a contrasting stain. This step can bring out specific features and add visual interest.

Step 9: Final Inspection

Conduct a final inspection after the finish has dried completely. Ensure that the wood's natural beauty is enhanced, and the finish has been applied uniformly.

Step 10: Sign or Mark Your Work (Optional)

If you haven't already, consider signing or marking your completed wood carving. This adds a personal touch and allows you to take pride in your creation.

Step 11: Display or Gift

Once your carving is finished and thoroughly dried, display it in a prominent place or consider gifting it to someone special. Appreciate the craftsmanship and effort you've put into creating a beautiful piece of art.

Adding finishing touches is a satisfying final step in the wood carving process. Each detail contributes to the overall aesthetic and ensures that your carving is a true reflection of your skill and creativity.

CHAPTER 5
Wood Carving Projects

Basic Whittled Spoon

Materials:

- Softwood block (e.g., pine or cedar)
- Carving knife
- Sandpaper (various grits)

Steps:

Prepare the Wood: Choose a softwood block and cut it into a rectangular shape, approximately 8-10 inches long and 2-3 inches wide.

Design the Spoon: Draw the outline of your spoon on one side of the wood. Keep the design simple for this beginner project.

Secure the Wood: Clamp the wood securely to a stable work surface, ensuring it won't move during carving.

Shape the Spoon Bowl: Carve out the spoon bowl using the carving knife. Start with shallow cuts, gradually increasing the depth. Work from the center outward.

Carve the Handle: Shape the handle of the spoon, keeping it comfortable to hold. Remove excess wood and refine the curves.

Smooth the Surface: Use sandpaper to smooth the entire surface of the spoon. Start with coarse grit and progress to finer grits for a polished finish.

Refine Details: Go back with the carving knife to refine any details and ensure the spoon is comfortable and aesthetically pleasing.

Finish (Optional): Apply a food-safe wood finish or mineral oil to protect the spoon if you plan to use it for eating. Follow the manufacturer's instructions.

Inspect and Enjoy: Inspect your whittled spoon for any rough spots or uneven areas.

Once satisfied, enjoy your handcrafted kitchen tool!

Whittled Keychain

Materials:

- Small hardwood block (e.g., oak or walnut)
- Carving knife
- Sandpaper (various grits)
- Keychain ring

Steps:

Prepare the Wood: Cut a small hardwood block, approximately 2-3 inches long and 1 inch wide.

Design the Keychain: Draw a simple design on one side of the wood. Consider shapes like hearts, animals, or initials for a personalized touch.

Secure the Wood: Clamp the wood securely to a stable work surface.

Carve the Design: Use the carving knife to carefully carve around the drawn design, removing excess wood to reveal the keychain shape.

Add Details: Refine your design by adding small details or carving textures. Keep the keychain lightweight and easy to carry.

Smooth the Surface: Sand the keychain using various grits of sandpaper. Ensure all edges are smooth and the surface is free of rough spots.

Punch a Hole: Using the carving knife or a small drill, create a hole near the top of the keychain for attaching the keychain ring.

Attach Keychain Ring: Insert the keychain ring through the hole. Ensure it's securely attached.

Finish (Optional): Apply a clear finish or leave the wood natural, depending on your preference.

Inspect and Use: Inspect your whittled keychain for any imperfections. Once satisfied, attach it to your keys or use it as a personalized accessory.

Whittled Bird

Materials:

- Softwood block (e.g., pine or cedar)
- Carving knife
- Sandpaper (various grits)

Steps:

Prepare the Wood: Choose a softwood block and cut it into a rectangular shape, approximately 6-8 inches long and 2 inches wide.

Design the Bird: Draw the outline of a simple bird on one side of the wood. Include features like wings, a beak, and tail feathers.

Secure the Wood: Clamp the wood securely to a stable work surface.

Carve the Outline: Use the carving knife to carefully carve around the drawn outline, defining the shape of the bird.

Shape the Features: Carve the wings, beak, and tail feathers, adding depth and dimension to your whittled bird.

Smooth the Surface: Sand the entire surface of the bird using various grits of sandpaper. Pay attention to details to achieve a polished finish.

Refine Details: Use the carving knife to refine any details and ensure a cohesive and appealing appearance.

Finish (Optional): Apply a clear finish or leave the wood natural, depending on your preference. This step enhances the overall look and provides protection.

Inspect and Display: Inspect your whittled bird for any rough spots or uneven areas. Once satisfied, display your handcrafted bird as a decorative piece.

Whittled Letter Opener

Materials:

- Medium hardwood block (e.g., cherry or maple)
- Carving knife
- Sandpaper (various grits)

Steps:

Prepare the Wood: Cut a medium-sized hardwood block, approximately 8-10 inches long and 1 inch wide.

Design the Letter Opener: Draw the outline of a sleek and simple letter opener shape on one side of the wood.

Secure the Wood: Clamp the wood securely to a stable work surface.

Carve the Outline: Use the carving knife to carve around the drawn outline, establishing the basic shape of the letter opener.

Define the Blade: Carve one end of the letter opener into a tapered blade shape. Pay attention to creating a sharp edge while maintaining safety.

Shape the Handle: Carve the opposite end into a comfortable handle shape, ensuring a grip-friendly design.

Smooth the Surface: Sand the entire surface of the letter opener, focusing on the blade and handle, using various grits of sandpaper.

Refine Details: Use the carving knife to refine any details on the blade and handle, ensuring a smooth and well-crafted finish.

Finish (Optional): Apply a clear finish or leave the wood natural, depending on your preference. Applying a finish can improve the visual appeal and provide protection for the wood.

Inspect and Use: Inspect your whittled letter opener for any imperfections. Once satisfied, use it as a functional and unique tool for opening letters.

These projects provide additional opportunities to hone your whittling skills and create charming, practical items. Remember to take your time, stay safe, and enjoy the creative process!

Relief Carved Flower

Materials:

- Medium hardwood block (e.g., cherry or maple)
- Carving gouges and chisels
- Mallet
- Sandpaper (various grits)

Steps:

Prepare the Wood: Cut a medium-sized hardwood block, approximately 6-8 inches square.

Design the Flower: Sketch the outline of a simple flower on one side of the wood. Consider petals, a center, and any additional details you'd like to include.

Secure the Wood: Clamp the wood securely to a stable work surface.

Outline the Flower: Use a fine carving tool to outline the main elements of the flower. This creates a guide for the deeper carving that will follow.

Carve Background: Carve away the background around the flower using carving gouges. Establish different levels within the design, creating depth.

Define Petals and Center: Use carving chisels and gouges to define the individual petals and the center of the flower. Add texture and details to enhance realism.

Smooth the Surface: Sand the entire surface of the relief carving, using various grits of sandpaper to achieve a smooth finish.

Refine Details: Use carving tools to refine any details on the petals and center of the flower. Smooth out curves and edges for a polished appearance.

Finish (Optional): Apply a clear finish or leave the wood natural, depending on your preference. Applying a finish can improve the visual appeal and provide protection for the wood.

Inspect and Display: Inspect your relief carved flower for any rough spots or uneven areas. Once satisfied, display your handcrafted flower as a decorative piece.

Relief Carved Celtic Knot

Materials:

- Medium hardwood block (e.g., oak or walnut)
- Carving gouges and chisels
- Mallet
- Sandpaper (various grits)

Steps:

Prepare the Wood: Cut a medium-sized hardwood block, approximately 8-10 inches square.

Design the Celtic Knot: Sketch the outline of a Celtic knot on one side of the wood. Start with a simple design, and as you gain experience, you can explore more complex knot patterns.

Secure the Wood: Clamp the wood securely to a stable work surface.

Outline the Knot: Use a fine carving tool to outline the main elements of the Celtic knot. This creates a guide for the deeper carving that will follow.

Carve Background: Carve away the background around the Celtic knot using carving gouges. Establish different levels within the design, creating depth.

Define Knot Elements: Use carving chisels and gouges to define the individual elements of the Celtic knot. Pay attention to the interweaving patterns and curves.

Smooth the Surface: Sand the entire surface of the relief carving, using various grits of sandpaper to achieve a smooth finish.

Refine Details: Use carving tools to refine any details within the Celtic knot. Ensure that the lines are crisp and the patterns are well-defined.

Finish (Optional): Apply a clear finish or leave the wood natural, depending on your preference. Applying a finish can improve the visual appeal and provide protection for the wood.

Inspect and Display: Inspect your relief carved Celtic knot for any imperfections. Once satisfied, display your handcrafted knot as a decorative piece or incorporate it into other projects.

Relief Carved Animal Silhouette

Materials:

- Medium hardwood block (e.g., cherry or walnut)
- Carving gouges and chisels
- Mallet
- Sandpaper (various grits)

Steps:

Prepare the Wood: Cut a medium-sized hardwood block, approximately 8-10 inches square.

Design the Animal Silhouette: Sketch the silhouette of your chosen animal on one side of the wood. Aim for a simple and recognizable shape.

Secure the Wood: Clamp the wood securely to a stable work surface.

Outline the Silhouette: Use a fine carving tool to outline the main elements of the animal silhouette. This creates a guide for the deeper carving that will follow.

Carve Background: Carve away the background around the animal silhouette using carving gouges. Establish different levels within the design, creating depth.

Define Animal Shape: Use carving chisels and gouges to define the contours of the animal silhouette. Pay attention to the natural curves and features of the chosen animal.

Add Details (Optional): If desired, add simple details to enhance the carving. Focus on key features that characterize the animal, such as ears, tail, or markings.

Smooth the Surface: Sand the entire surface of the relief carving, using various grits of sandpaper to achieve a smooth finish.

Refine Details: Use carving tools to refine any details on the animal silhouette.

Ensure that the lines are crisp, and the overall form is well-defined.

Finish (Optional): Apply a clear finish or leave the wood natural, depending on your preference. Applying a finish can improve the visual appeal and provide protection for the wood.

Inspect and Display: Inspect your relief carved animal silhouette for any rough spots or uneven areas. Once satisfied, display your handcrafted piece as a decorative element.

Relief Carved Sunburst Design

Materials:

- Medium hardwood block (e.g., oak or maple)
- Carving gouges and chisels

- Mallet
- Sandpaper (various grits)

Steps:

Prepare the Wood: Cut a medium-sized hardwood block, approximately 8-10 inches square.

Design the Sunburst: Sketch a sunburst design on one side of the wood. This can include rays radiating from a central point.

Secure the Wood: Clamp the wood securely to a stable work surface.

Outline the Sunburst: Use a fine carving tool to outline the main elements of the sunburst design. This creates a guide for the deeper carving that will follow.

Carve Background: Carve away the background around the sunburst using carving gouges. Establish different levels within the design, creating depth.

Define Rays and Center: Use carving chisels and gouges to define the individual rays of the sunburst. Create varying depths to add visual interest. Define the central point.

Add Textures (Optional): If desired, add textures to the rays or the central area to create contrast and dimension.

Smooth the Surface: Sand the entire surface of the relief carving, using various grits of sandpaper to achieve a smooth finish.

Refine Details: Use carving tools to refine any details in the sunburst design. Ensure that the lines are crisp and the overall pattern is well-executed.

Finish (Optional): Apply a clear finish or leave the wood natural, depending on your preference. Applying a finish can improve the visual appeal and provide protection for the wood.

Inspect and Display: Inspect your relief carved sunburst design for any imperfections. Once satisfied, display your handcrafted piece as a decorative element, perhaps as wall art.

These relief carving projects offer a variety of themes and styles, allowing you to explore different techniques and create visually engaging carvings. Enjoy the process and showcase your finished pieces with pride!

Chip Carved Coaster

Materials:

- Small hardwood square (e.g., basswood or cherry)
- Chip carving knife
- Pencil
- Ruler
- Sandpaper (various grits)

Steps:

Prepare the Wood: Cut a small hardwood square, approximately 4x4 inches, for your coaster.

Design the Pattern: Draw a simple geometric pattern on one side of the wood using a pencil and ruler. Consider classic chip carving motifs like triangles or diamonds.

Secure the Wood: Clamp the wood securely to a stable work surface.

Outline the Design: Use the chip carving knife to carefully outline the main elements of your design. These lines will guide your chip cuts.

Make Chip Cuts: Begin making small chip cuts along the outlined areas, removing triangular pieces of wood. Take your time and maintain consistent angles.

Continue Carving: Work your way through the entire design, creating the chip-carved pattern. Focus on achieving clean, crisp cuts for an intricate look.

Smooth the Surface: Sand the entire surface of the chip-carved coaster using various grits of sandpaper to achieve a smooth finish.

Refine Details: Use the chip carving knife to refine any details and ensure the edges of the cuts are sharp and well-defined.

Finish (Optional): Apply a clear finish or leave the wood natural, depending on your preference. Applying a finish can improve the visual appeal and provide protection for the wood.

Inspect and Use: Inspect your chip-carved coaster for any rough spots or uneven areas. Once satisfied, use it as a functional and decorative piece.

Chip Carved Wooden Box Lid

Materials:

- Wooden box with a flat lid (e.g., pine or cedar)
- Chip carving knife
- Pencil
- Ruler
- Sandpaper (various grits)

Steps:

Prepare the Wood: Select a wooden box with a flat lid. Pine or cedar are suitable choices.

Design the Chip Carving: Sketch a chip carving design on the lid using a pencil and ruler. Choose a pattern that complements the size and shape of the lid.

Secure the Box: Secure the wooden box in a stable position using clamps or by holding it firmly.

Outline the Design: Use the chip carving knife to outline the main elements of your design on the box lid. These lines will guide your chip cuts.

Make Chip Cuts: Begin making chip cuts along the outlined areas, removing small triangular pieces of wood. Pay attention to maintaining consistent angles for a cohesive look.

Continue Carving: Work your way through the entire design, creating the chip-carved pattern on the lid. Take breaks as needed to ensure precision.

Smooth the Surface: Sand the entire surface of the chip-carved box lid using various grits of sandpaper to achieve a smooth finish.

Refine Details: Use the chip carving knife to refine any details and ensure the edges of the cuts are sharp and well-defined.

Finish (Optional): Apply a clear finish or leave the wood natural, depending on your preference. Applying a finish can improve the visual appeal and provide protection for the wood.

Inspect and Assemble: Inspect your chip-carved box lid for any imperfections. Once satisfied, assemble the box and use it for storage or as a decorative piece.

Chip Carved Wooden Spoon Handle

Materials:

- Wooden spoon (unfinished)
- Chip carving knife
- Pencil
- Ruler
- Sandpaper (various grits)

Steps:

Prepare the Wooden Spoon: Begin with an unfinished wooden spoon. Ensure that the spoon handle is flat and suitable for carving.

Design the Chip Carving: Sketch a chip carving design on the handle using a pencil and ruler. Choose a pattern that complements the shape and size of the handle.

Secure the Spoon: Secure the wooden spoon in a stable position using clamps or by holding it firmly.

Outline the Design: Use the chip carving knife to outline the main elements of your design on the spoon handle. These lines will guide your chip cuts.

Make Chip Cuts: Begin making chip cuts along the outlined areas, removing small triangular pieces of wood. Focus on maintaining consistent angles for a cohesive appearance.

Continue Carving: Work your way through the entire design, creating the chip-carved pattern on the spoon handle. Pay attention to the contours of the handle for a comfortable grip.

Smooth the Surface: Sand the entire surface of the chip-carved spoon handle using various grits of sandpaper to achieve a smooth finish.

Refine Details: Use the chip carving knife to refine any details and ensure the edges of the cuts are sharp and well-defined.

Finish (Optional): Apply a clear finish or leave the wood natural, depending on your preference. Applying a finish can improve the visual appeal and provide protection for the wood.

Inspect and Use: Inspect your chip-carved wooden spoon handle for any imperfections. Once satisfied, use it for cooking or as a decorative kitchen item.

Chip Carved Decorative Plate

Materials:

- Unfinished wooden plate
- Chip carving knife
- Pencil
- Ruler
- Sandpaper (various grits)

Steps:

Prepare the Wooden Plate: Begin with an unfinished wooden plate. Ensure that the plate surface is flat and suitable for carving.

Design the Chip Carving: Sketch a chip carving design on the plate using a pencil and ruler. Consider creating a border or a central motif that complements the shape of the plate.

Secure the Plate: Secure the wooden plate in a stable position using clamps or by holding it firmly.

Outline the Design: Use the chip carving knife to outline the main elements of your design on the plate. These lines will guide your chip cuts.

Make Chip Cuts: Begin making chip cuts along the outlined areas, removing small triangular pieces of wood. Pay attention to creating a balanced and visually appealing pattern.

Continue Carving: Work your way through the entire design, creating the chip-carved pattern on the plate. Consider incorporating varying depths for added interest.

Smooth the Surface: Sand the entire surface of the chip-carved plate using various grits of sandpaper to achieve a smooth finish.

Refine Details: Use the chip carving knife to refine any details and ensure the edges of the cuts are sharp and well-defined.

Finish (Optional): Apply a clear finish or leave the wood natural, depending on your preference. Applying a finish can improve the visual appeal and provide protection for the wood.

Inspect and Display: Inspect your chip-carved decorative plate for any imperfections. Once satisfied, display it as a unique piece of functional art.

These chip carving projects offer a blend of creativity and practicality, allowing you to add personalized touches to everyday items. Enjoy the process of chip carving and showcase your finished pieces with pride!

CHAPTER 6
Troubleshooting

If you encounter issues while wood carving, here are some common troubleshooting tips to help you address and overcome challenges:

1. Wood Splitting or Splintering:

Solution: Check the wood's moisture content; overly dry or wet wood can lead to splitting. Use wood with proper moisture levels. If splitting persists, adjust your carving technique, ensuring your tools are sharp and that you follow the wood grain.

2. Uneven Surface or Rough Edges:

Solution: Sand the carved surface using progressively finer grits of sandpaper. Ensure your carving tools are sharp and make controlled, consistent cuts. Practice maintaining a steady hand and smooth movements during carving.

3. Difficulty Controlling Depth of Cut:

Solution: Practice controlled cutting techniques. Use a light grip on the carving tools, allowing for better control. Gradually increase the depth of your cuts, and periodically check your progress to avoid carving too deeply.

4. Tools Not Cutting Efficiently:

Solution: Ensure your carving tools are sharp. Regularly sharpen and hone the edges using a sharpening stone or strop. Dull tools can lead to frustration and imprecise cuts.

5. Chip Breakage or Tear-Out:

Solution: Adjust the angle and pressure of your cuts. Pay attention to the direction of the wood grain and make cuts in the same direction. Use a proper carving technique, employing a slicing motion rather than hacking at the wood.

6. Design Not Transferring Well:

Solution: Use a clear and defined design on the wood. Ensure proper transfer methods like tracing or carbon paper. If lines are faint, go over them with a pencil to make them more visible.

7. Difficulty Achieving Fine Details:

Solution: Choose the right carving tools for the job. Utilize smaller, specialized tools for intricate details. Practice patience and take your time when working on fine details.

8. Wood Grain Tear-Out:

Solution: Pay close attention to the direction of the wood grain. Carve in the same direction as the grain to minimize tear-out. Adjust your cutting technique to accommodate changes in grain direction.

9. Inconsistent Tool Marks:

Solution: Maintain a consistent angle and pressure when making cuts. Practice control and use a rhythmic carving motion. Check your tools for any irregularities or damage.

10. Lack of Confidence or Skill:

Solution: Practice regularly to improve your carving skills. Begin with easy projects and incrementally advance to more intricate ones. Seek guidance from experienced carvers, and consider taking a carving class or workshop.

Remember, wood carving is a skill that improves with practice. Don't be discouraged by challenges; instead, view them as opportunities to learn and refine your technique. Patience, attention to detail, and a willingness to adapt will contribute to your success as a wood carver.

General Tips

1. Start with the Right Wood: Choose softwoods like pine or basswood for beginners; they're easier to carve. As you gain experience, explore hardwoods like oak or walnut for more intricate projects.

2. Use Sharp Tools: Regularly sharpen your carving tools to ensure clean and precise cuts. A sharp tool makes carving more enjoyable and helps prevent accidents.

3. Understand Wood Grain: Pay attention to the direction of the wood grain. Carve with the grain to minimize tear-out and achieve smoother surfaces.

4. Practice Safety First: Wear appropriate safety gear, including gloves and safety glasses. Always carve away from yourself and be aware of your surroundings to prevent accidents.

5. Master Basic Techniques: Start with basic carving techniques like push cuts, pull cuts, and stop cuts. Practice these foundational skills to build your carving proficiency.

6. Start Simple: Begin with straightforward projects to build confidence. Gradually take on more complex designs as your skills improve.

7. Use a Strop for Tool Maintenance: Keep your tools sharp by using a strop regularly. Stropping helps maintain the edge and prolongs the life of your carving tools.

8. Work in a Well-Lit Space: Carving requires attention to detail. Ensure you have ample lighting to clearly see your work and avoid mistakes.

9. Plan Your Design: Sketch your design on paper before starting to carve. Having a clear plan helps prevent mistakes and ensures a more successful outcome.

10. Control Depth of Cut: Learn to control the depth of your cuts. Start with shallow cuts and gradually increase depth as needed. This prevents unintended removal of too much material.

11. Embrace Mistakes as Learning Opportunities: Mistakes are part of the learning process. Instead of getting discouraged, use them as opportunities to refine your skills and techniques.

12. Take Breaks: Wood carving requires concentration. Ensure to take breaks periodically to avoid fatigue and sustain concentration.

13. Invest in Quality Tools: While starting with basic tools is fine, consider investing in higher-quality tools as you progress. Investing in high-quality tools can greatly enhance your carving experience.

14. Explore Different Carving Styles: Experiment with various carving styles, such as relief carving, chip carving, or whittling. Each style offers a unique set of challenges and rewards.

15. Join Carving Communities: Connect with other wood carvers online or in local communities. Share experiences, seek advice, and learn from others in the carving community.

16. Protect Your Hands: Use carving gloves to protect your hands from accidental slips or cuts. They offer an extra layer of protection.

17. Enjoy the Process: Wood carving is a creative and meditative activity. Enjoy the process, and don't rush. Take pride in your progress and finished projects.

Remember that wood carving is a skill that develops over time. Maintain patience, persevere, and take time to acknowledge and celebrate your accomplishments throughout the journey. Whether you carve for relaxation or create intricate pieces of art, the journey is as important as the destination.

CONCLUSION

In conclusion, wood carving is a rewarding and versatile craft that offers a blend of artistic expression and practical skill. As you embark on your carving journey, remember the importance of patience, practice, and continuous learning. Starting with simple projects allows you to build a solid foundation, while gradually taking on more complex designs expands your repertoire.

The choice of wood, maintaining sharp tools, and understanding wood grain are crucial aspects that contribute to successful carving. Safety should always be a priority, with proper gear and carving techniques to minimize risks. Mistakes are inevitable, but they provide valuable learning opportunities, shaping you into a more proficient carver.

Exploring different carving styles, joining carving communities, and seeking inspiration from fellow enthusiasts can enhance your experience and foster a sense of camaraderie. Remember that the process of carving is as fulfilling as the finished piece, so take breaks, enjoy the meditative nature of the craft, and appreciate the unique beauty that each project brings.

Whether you're creating functional items or intricate works of art, wood carving allows you to leave a personal mark on your creations. As you progress, embrace the challenges, celebrate your successes, and let the natural beauty of wood come to life through your skilled hands. May your wood carving journey be both enjoyable and fulfilling, as you craft pieces that reflect your creativity and dedication to this timeless craft. Happy carving!